Blessings from Being BULLIED

*My Journey of Empowerment
and Unexpected Transformation by*

CHRISTINA RONDEAU

DEDICATION

This heartfelt book is dedicated to all those who have experienced the painful impact of bullying in their lives. I want you to know that there is always hope, and I encourage you to keep pushing forward. Remember, never let anyone diminish your inner strength and power. May this book serve as a source of inspiration and upliftment, reminding you that you are not alone and that a brighter tomorrow awaits.

© 2023 Christina Rondeau
All rights reserved. No part of this publication
may be reproduced, stored in a retrieval system, or transmitted,
in any form, or by any means, electronic, mechanical, photocopying,
recording, or otherwise, without the prior consent of the publisher.

Table of
CONTENTS

Forward …………………………………………………… vii

Introduction ……………………………………………… xiii

Chapter 1: The Sneeze …………………………………… 1

Chapter 2: The New School ……………………………… 7

Chapter 3: The Bus ……………………………………… 15

Chapter 4: The Stance …………………………………… 23

Chapter 5: The Hallway ………………………………… 29

Chapter 6: The Locker …………………………………… 37

Chapter 7: The Cemetary ………………………………… 43

Chapter 8: Rocky ………………………………………… 49

Chapter 9: Bye-Bye Bully ………………………………… 55

Chapter 10: My Bully's Blessings to Me ………………… 61

Bullying …………………………………………………… 67

Bullying Information Sheet to Help Parents …………… 73

Blessings from Being

BULLIED

*My Journey of Empowerment
and Unexpected Transformation by*

CHRISTINA RONDEAU

FORWARD

In the world of *Blessings from Being Bullied*, embark on an inspiring journey of resilience and transformation. This captivating memoir takes you through the life of a remarkable individual who turned adversity into opportunity, showing us the hidden blessings that can emerge from the most challenging experiences.

With raw honesty and unwavering courage, the author shares their personal encounters with bullying, revealing the profound impact it had on their life. But this isn't just a tale of victimhood; it's a testament to the power of the human spirit to rise above adversity and find strength in the face of cruelty.

Through their remarkable journey, the author uncovers the invaluable life lessons hidden within the shadows of bullying. With each hardship, they discovered untapped wells of inner resilience, compassion, and self-discovery. From these experiences, they forged an unbreakable spirit and cultivated a profound understanding of empathy and kindness.

Blessings from Being Bullied is not merely a memoir; it is a guidebook for anyone who has ever faced bullying or adversity in any form. Drawing on their own triumphs and setbacks, the author offers practical advice, empowering strategies, and heartfelt encouragement for those seeking to navigate the treacherous waters of bullying.

BLESSINGS FROM BEING BULLIED

Prepare to be inspired, uplifted, and moved to action as you delve into this captivating account of triumph over torment. *Blessings from Being Bullied* is a testament to the indomitable human spirit and a reminder that even in our darkest moments, there are blessings waiting to be discovered.

INTRODUCTION

Initially, my intention was to craft a simple resource for parents. However, as I delved deeper into the subject, I felt an overwhelming desire to share my personal journey. My own encounter with a bully was transformative, forging me into the person I am today. Fortunately, I count myself among the few who can frame their experience in such a light. The unsettling truth is that countless children grapple with bullying every single day. During the school year, I receive numerous calls each week from distraught parents seeking assistance and wanting to enroll their children in a kids' kickboxing program so they can defend themselves. Their desperation is palpable, a feeling I, as a parent, understand all too well. Our greatest fear is that a bully might drive our child to the brink of despair, potentially leading to suicide or leaving lasting scars that can disrupt their future.

Bullying narratives are abundant. Tales of families relocating, switching schools or entire cities, hoping to elude the torment, only to encounter it elsewhere. Bullying isn't something you can simply run away from. Instead, our primary focus should be to instill values in our children, guiding them to neither become bullies nor victims. I genuinely believe that introducing children to the disciplines of martial arts. What I teach, reality self-defense and kickboxing, mix it all together. This can play a pivotal role in their upbringing. It fosters etiquette, respect, discipline, and goal setting, virtues that inevitably resonate within the home environment. Martial arts doesn't just provide self-defense techniques; it empowers individuals with confidence, from young children to senior citizens. It equips them with tools to defend themselves against potential threats, emphasizing the importance of safety and stranger awareness.

Reflecting on my youth, having graduated high school in 1990, I recall an era devoid of cell phones and dominated by cassette tapes. Cyberbullying and online harassment were alien concepts. Today's youth, however, don't have the luxury of disconnecting. Bullying is omnipresent, shadowing them incessantly through social media and digital platforms. Parents must grasp the magnitude of the emotional weight their children carry. Dismissing it as a minor issue is a grave error; for these kids, it's monumental. It's paramount for parents to approach their children with empathy, compassion, and open ears. Sometimes just holding space for your children and listening is the best thing a parent can do for them.

In conclusion, I urge you to be proactive. Arm your children with the skills and self-assurance they require to navigate today's challenging landscape. Equip them now, before they find themselves confronting a bully and you find yourself wishing you enrolled them in a program to learn how to defend themselves sooner.

~Christina

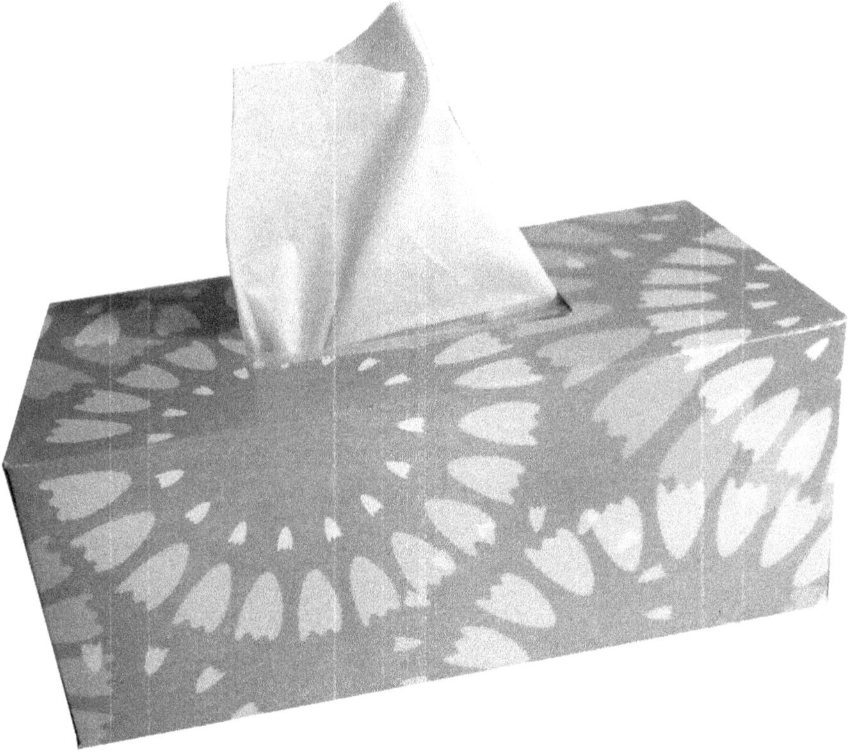

CHAPTER 1
THE SNEEZE

New England allergies. You can't escape them. As a child, I was allergic to the Earth. Every season brought a new "weed," and my allergies just couldn't get under control. Allergy shots every week, allergy meds every day, and still I would have sneezing attacks throughout the day. I was in 4th grade, and Ms. Pickering was one of my teachers. We rotated between two classes in 4th grade, and Ms. Pickering's was the class no one looked forward to going to. Ms. Pickering was in her 40's, tall, lean, with short dark hair, and a very stern voice. Ms. Pickering wasn't soft or compassionate; she was like a drill instructor, and we feared her more than we liked her. It was the middle of class, and I felt it coming on like a freight train. I tried so hard to hold it in. I had a little pack of tissues my mom packed in my backpack, but the backpack was in my homeroom class. There was no stopping this sneeze and as hard as I tried to hold it in, I just couldn't. The sneeze exploded out of me. It was so loud, and I was so embarrassed. The room was so quiet prior to my sneeze you could hear a pin drop, and the sneeze jolted everyone in the room. All my classmates looked up and I quietly said, "Excuse me."

Suddenly I heard, "Ms. Rondeau! Stand up!" Ms. Pickering was yelling at me. I looked around, hoping someone would save me from the wrath of this mean woman but no such luck. I rose from my seat and just stood there. "Walk up here now!" yelled Ms. Pickering.

I followed directions and walked up to her desk. I was shaking, wondering why she was mad at me for sneezing, and nothing could be worse for me than being embarrassed in front of a classroom of my friends and peers. The aisle to her desk was long. I walked slowly, and it took me an eternity to get there. I felt sick over it, and I was fighting back the tears. I stood in front of her, shaking with tears in my eyes. I just stood there.

"Are you going to cry? You come out here now." She said pointing to outside the classroom door. I walked outside the door and tears rolled down my face. Outside the door, we were in the hall. It was empty, and she left the classroom door open halfway and proceeded to scream at me for sneezing in her classroom. I don't recall exactly what she said but I remember watching Mrs. Jolly walk out of her class to see what was going on. Ms. Pickering grabbed my face when I turned to look at Ms. Jolly and continued to scream at me about sneezing and told me not to look away when she was talking to me. At some point she told me to go back to my seat, which I did. I zoned out. I was a whole bunch of feelings at this point. I remember some friends consoling me after the bell rang, and I was very thankful I didn't have her class anymore the rest of that day.

Later that night at home, I didn't even have to tell my mom what had happened because Mrs. Jolly had already called her. Mrs. Jolly's husband was a police officer who worked with my dad (also a police officer), and after she told her husband what happened he told her to call and tell my mom right away. Apparently, Ms. Pickering was laughing about it in the teacher's room, and Mrs. Jolly asked her what happened, since she also witnessed it herself. Ms. Pickering told her basically, she picked on me for sneezing.

My mom stormed into the school the next day and was so upset she pulled me out of 4th grade on the spot and put me in a different school for 5th grade. I was so sad to leave my friends, but my mom was trying to protect me from this teacher. What we didn't know was the new school was going to be my introduction to bullies.

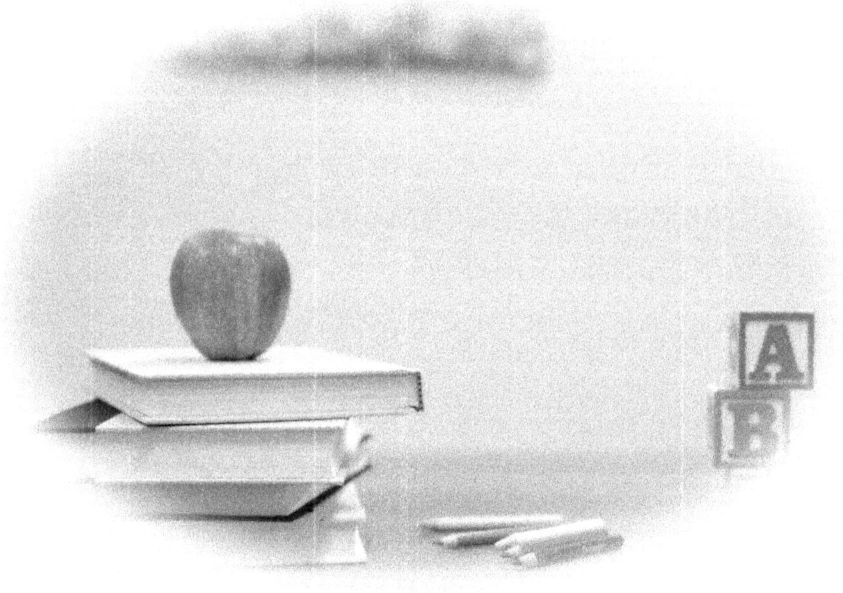
A
B

CHAPTER 2
THE NEW SCHOOL

The new school was on the other side of the city. I didn't know anyone, and it was scary walking into a new school and having to create new friendships and to try and fit in. The teachers were great, and I made some new friends, but I was targeted. I was targeted by one group of kids for my nice clothes. I was called "rich," and they didn't like the police, which meant they didn't like me because my dad was a police officer. For the most part I ignored this group of kids, but toward the end of the year it became bad.

One particular girl, Denise, realized I wasn't going to fight back if she physically pushed me around, and at some point, she just didn't care what happened to her. One day she decided she wanted my pink satin Cheryl Ladd, Charlie's Angels jacket. This jacket was my favorite jacket, and she wanted it. It was recess, and she came over with her crew of boys and told me to take my jacket off. I refused so she grabbed at me and pulled the sleeve of my jacket. I pulled away, so she grabbed my arm and gave my head a shove. She let go of my arm and I went flying. The boys pointed and laughed at me, and I shook it off, got up, and wondered why the teachers looking right at us did nothing. To this day I will never understand how the teachers at recess were oblivious to everything that was going on right in front of them. This recess bullying went on every day for weeks. I stopped wearing my jacket to school after that day, but no matter what I wore, she wanted it. I avoided her at recess, but it was impossible. She was so aggressive, and she just picked on me at every opportunity. One day I was walking near the baseball field at recess, and I was far from the teachers on this day (not that they did anything anyway). This was the day Denise had decided she was going to take the jacket I had on and beat me up. I saw her coming at me with her crew of boys, and I had nowhere to run. She cornered me against the baseball fence and her crew of boys were on the other side of the fence behind me. She pushed me against the fence, and the boys kicked me in the back as I crashed into the fence.

It was horrifying.

I didn't know how to fight, and I just had to take this beating. I gave her the jacket I had on, and she still wanted to hurt me. Just when I thought this push and kick beating would never end, an angel appeared. This tall, heavy-set girl named Mary came to my rescue. She stood behind me and let the boys kick her instead and screamed at Daniel to stop. Mary was yelling loudly, and it finally drew the attention of some teachers who slowly came walking towards us to see what was going on. Mary and I told them what happened, and we all had to go to the office.

I was cut up and bleeding, so it was a trip to the nurse for me first. My mom was called in, and Daniel was suspended for a day. This made things worse because now I was a tattle tale, and Denise would call me this name till the end of the school year.

After this incident, every time my mom would pick me up, this group of kids would stalk me. They would walk behind me as I went to parent pick up, mumbling nasty stuff. They would mouth off to my mother; one girl even called my mother names I won't even repeat.

We even saw this group of kids at a local baseball game and the things they said to my mom were disgraceful. My mom decided the kids at this school weren't very nice and back to my old school I went for 6th grade.

Thank goodness.

The next few years were great. I had my friends back, and most of them all went to the same middle school. The middle school was rough, a melting pot of the city's kids from all over. I was thankfully no bully's target during middle school. I escaped 6th-11th grade with no issues and truly enjoyed school, sports, and my friendships. I am still BFFs with friends from elementary school and middle school. We have experienced all of life's ups and downs together. We even raised our children together and get together several times throughout the year. I am truly blessed with these friendships and wish other kids could be as fortunate.

Fast forward to my senior year in high school. I almost escaped high school with no bully and a pretty perfect memory of positive experiences. Until she came along.

The bully.

SCHOOL BUS

FAIRVIEW

CHAPTER 3

THE BUS

It was a crisp, fall day in New England. I was only 17 years old and in my senior year of high school. I was popular, a jock, and had a lot of friends. I walked into the school with a weight on my chest. I was nervous, and I felt scared. I looked around and my eyes searched for her; it felt like my eyes were in a race, rapidly looking past each kid, trying to see through them and bend around the corners, racing to find her before she would find me. If I could spot her, it would give me a chance to not make eye contact or pass her in the hall. It would give me time to turn and go the other direction. She was making my life a nightmare.

Her, the bully, I won't even give a name because I nothing her. The bully decided to bully me on the bus on the way home from a track meet one day. It was the first time she picked on me. I was hoping it was the last. We used to be friends; back in 6th grade we even had matching best friend necklaces. She would come over on the bus after school and play in my yard, eat dinner, and my mom would bring her home later that night. She lived in the projects and her family had their struggles. By the time we entered 7th grade and a new school, middle school, we were mixed with hundreds of kids from all over the city. There were 7th, 8th, and 9th graders in this school and the school was a little rough. Immediately she found new friends and we just faded apart. Nothing ever happened, we said, "hello" and joked around when we saw each other. She was in a few of my classes, and we played sports together some seasons.

Fast forward to 12th grade, and on the bus home from a track meet, it was loud with kids talking, mixed boys and girls. It was dark out and a little cold. We were bundled up in our sweat suits and just talking about the track meet. The bully was sitting in front of me. She suddenly sat up in her seat and turned around. She looked at me and started verbally picking on me about my hair, making fun of my ponytail on top of my head and the scrunchie holding my hair together. After talking about it and laughing at me, while getting others to look at my "funny ponytail" too, she started grabbing at it, tugging and pulling at my hair. I slapped her hand away and right away, she started with fighting comments.

"Oh, you wanna play like that and slap my hand?" she said in a tough, mean, aggressive tone.

"I don't want you pulling my hair," I stated.

"Well, what you gonna do now? You gonna punch me if I do it again?" she said.

"No, I am going to push your hand away again because I don't want you touching me," I said.

By this time, some boys on the bus were all egging her on to pull my hair, and a few mutual friends around us were laughing but not exactly stopping this nonsense.

"Yeah, push my hand away again, and I will lay you out!" she screamed in my face.

I decided to look away and not to engage her.

A few minutes went by, and she tried to argue with me again. "What! Ya going to cry? Go cry to Mommy.. ooooohh she picked on me. Wahhh, wahhhh," she said.

"What's your problem? We are friends. What's your issue with me right now?" I asked.

"I don't like you!" she yelled in my face.

"Why? What have I ever done to you? You used to be my BFF. We played together, and you would come over. We haven't hung out in years, and now suddenly, you don't like me?" I said.

"I don't need a reason! I just don't like you!" she yelled. She screamed in my face as she took her hand and flicked me on the side of the head.

That was it… I now had a bully.

I didn't even say anything back or react to the flick; I just turned my head and looked out the window and sat there in silence. I was suddenly so afraid to get beat up by her. She also had a crew of these new friends who were just as mean. They loved to fight, and the fights were brutal. They didn't stop once they hit people. They would slam their heads on the ground over and over, kick them in the face, body, and wherever else. They were mean and aggressive, and they would all jump in. That fear went through me, and suddenly this feeling overcame me, and it was very scary.

The bus couldn't have dropped me off fast enough. I stuck near some other friends and walked to my car. I drove right home, went into my bedroom, and just cried. I was so frustrated; I just didn't understand where this was coming from and why she had suddenly turned on me. I literally did nothing to this person, and as she said herself, she had no reason, she "just didn't like me."

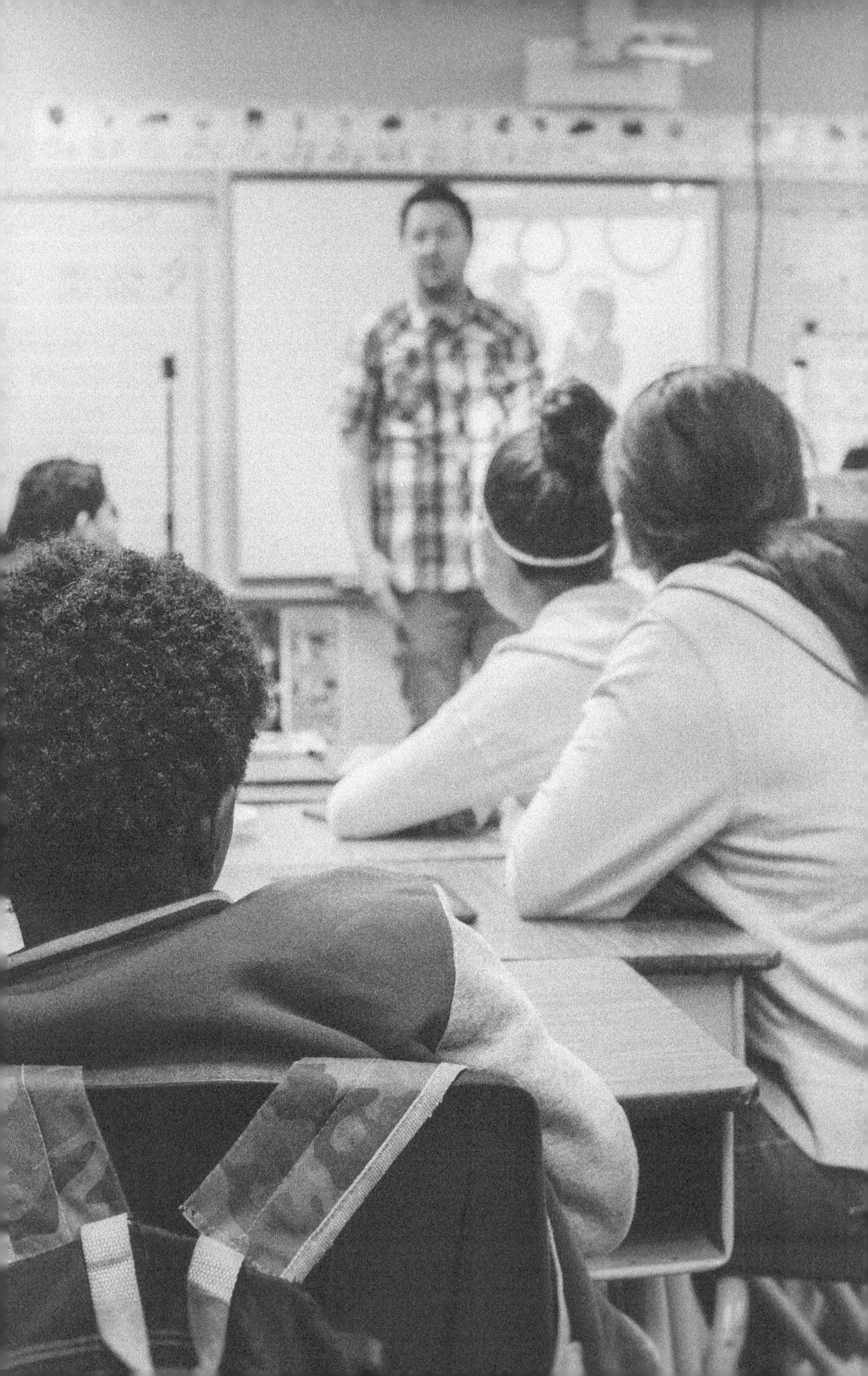

CHAPTER 4
THE STANCE

The next day I headed into school and tried not to think about it. It was consuming my thoughts, but I had to focus on my schoolwork. I talked to my friends who weren't on the track team or on the bus about the incident and they all agreed I just became her target for no reason. My friends were amazing but not tough nor fighters in any way. I had one particular friend who always had my back. She was a little bit of a bully herself at times, but she was the only one I could go to that I knew would jump in or protect me if need be. We would have nice long bells in between classes. Before I was so scared of this bully, I enjoyed the long time between classes and would laugh with friends and hang out at my locker. We would pass notes and make plans for after school.

I decided to go find Sally and tell her what happened in case anything else continued with the bully. Sally was over near the boys' lockers and being her crazy little self. Sally had a loud personality, and the minute I told her, she was ready to go find the bully and fight her. I did not encourage that at all and wanted nothing to do with the bully, but I wanted Sally to keep her ears open and have my back in case anything happened.

I headed over to English class and was finally not thinking about the bully and just doing my work. That's when I saw her. An eerie feeling washed over me. I felt like someone was staring at me; it was strange. I looked up from my paper and gazed around the classroom. As my eyes looked over to the right, I saw her. She was staring in the classroom through the window in the door. I made eye contact with her, and she pointed right at me. It wasn't a fun point or happy point. It was an "I am going to f you up" point. If you have ever been pointed at by someone like this, then you know what I am talking about. My stomach dropped. I suddenly felt nauseous and looked away. I looked down at my paper and started to write. I was sick to my stomach.

What the hell was I going to do? I started to write a note to my buddy, Erin, who was sitting next to me. I told her what just happened. She read it then looked up at me and gave me the "oh shit you're in trouble" face, then wrote me a note back. I decided to stay close to Erin after class when walking to the next class and that was the moment school changed for me.

I now walked the halls in fear. I was instantly anxious, and I had chest pains that felt like an elephant was sitting on top of me. I didn't even want to go to my locker. I wanted to quickly walk right to my class and just get in there and sit down. I felt like I was safe if I was in class, and she couldn't get me. I was praying a teacher would stop the attack if she tried to beat me up and hopefully, I wouldn't get too beaten up. Then I started to think about all my friends watching me get beat up. That would be awful. The boys would think it was funny and would probably laugh and cheer her on. I think anyone scared of her would cheer her on to so she wouldn't pick on them.

I decided to skip track that day and went right home after school. I didn't want to see her at track practice, so I avoided that. I also knew if I told the coach I didn't go because of this bully, he would say something to her, and that would make this all 100 times worse.

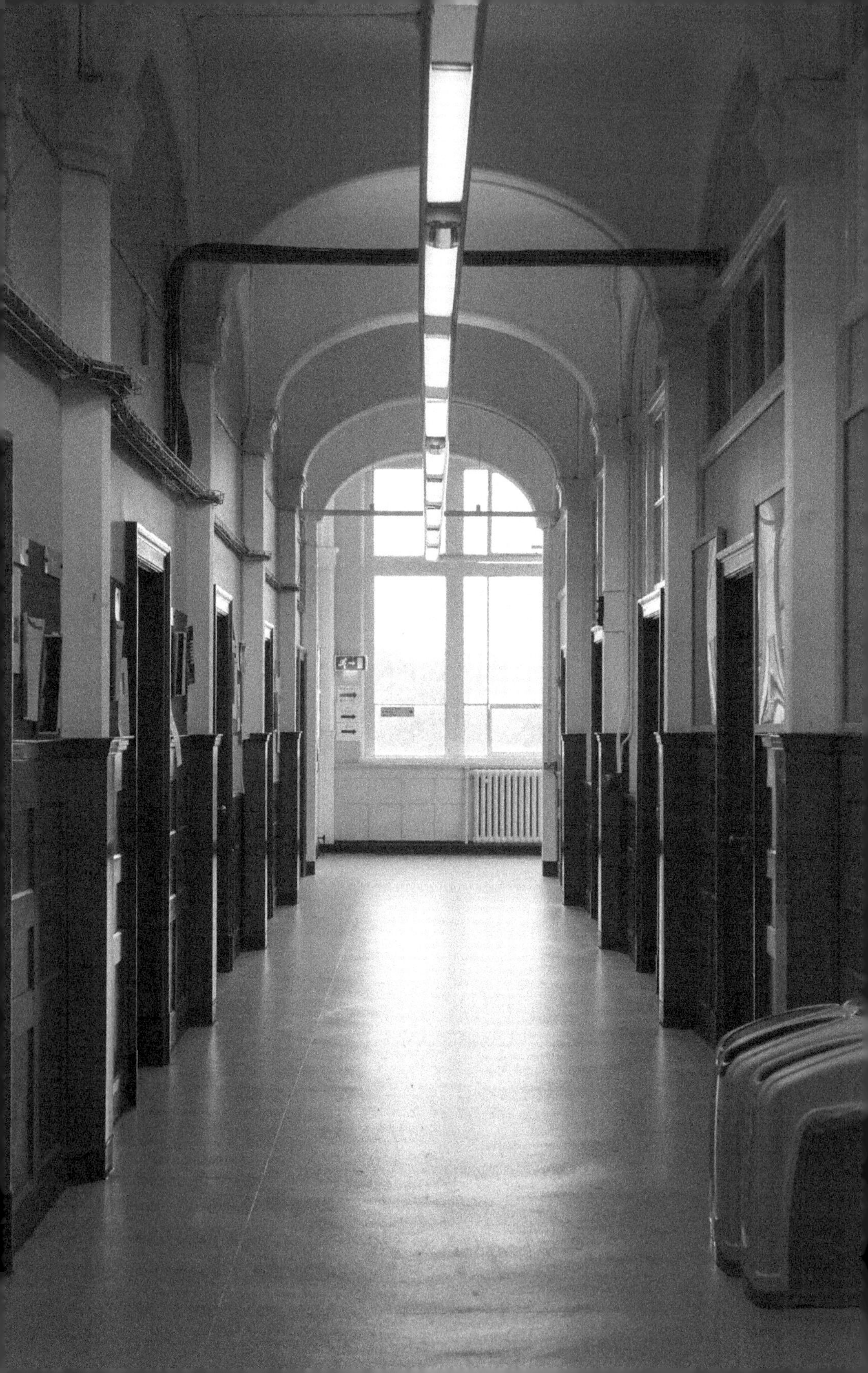

CHAPTER 5
THE HALLWAY

A few days went by, and I avoided the bully at all costs. I decided to say my knee hurt and had my mom tell the coach I couldn't run. I was lying to everyone about why I didn't go to track. I was good too; I was a 100-meter all-star and long-distance champ. I loved the long jump and the hurdles. I had run cross country and track since 7th grade. I made a name for myself with cross country and the 100-meter dash. It sucked that I had to avoid track in my senior year because of this bully. We were at the end of track season, and I had nothing in me to go back unless the bully wasn't targeting me anymore.

I was cautious at school. I continued to just go to class and avoid the lockers or lingering in the hallway with friends. I would spot her from a distance and always go the other way. I didn't even go to the bathroom when needed. I would hold it all day because I was afraid of her trapping me in there. I didn't realize this at the time, but this stress was taking a toll on my physical health.

A couple of weeks went by, and I would always ask my good friends if the bully was in school or if they saw her. She wasn't in school for a little while and I remember the relief I felt. I let my guard down one day and went to my locker, and like a scene out of a scary movie, I closed my locker door and there she was. Her face was right there; it was so scary and so shocking at the same time.

She flicked me right in the head and said, "Where is your ponytail today?"

"Haha." I made some strange sound, a cross between a laugh, chuckle, and scared, fearful sound. I turned my back to her and walked away towards my class, praying she wasn't going to hit me from behind.

"Yeah, walk away. I am gonna get you!" she yelled.

Get me?! What the hell? I thought as I walked to my class, my eyes filled up with water and fighting the tears back. I sat in my next class, zoned out. I didn't hear a thing the teacher said; I just kept thinking over and over, Why is she doing this and how do I get her to stop? I was scribbling on my notebook, drawing little palm trees over and over, when I felt it again, the eerie feeling, like someone was staring me down. I was afraid to look up, so I kept scribbling and drawing nervous little doodles. I peeked out the corner of my eye while my head was down, and I saw her. This time the door to the class was open and she was staring there in the doorway. Her arms were folded, and she was leaning against the wall. She was just staring at me. God knows how long, but I felt it. I didn't look at her. I kept drawing. Then I heard her yell, "I am gonna get you!" She screamed it. Everyone looked out the door and they could see her walking away. The teacher went to the door and closed it, not realizing what was going on. A few kids looked at me. I just looked away.

Did they know? Was it obvious now and going around the school that she was going to get me? This is awful. *This is my senior year of high school. I am supposed to be having the best year ever. She is making this awful for me*, I thought.

I went home and quit track.

I wanted to quit school too, but my mom wouldn't allow that. I also didn't want my parents to know what was going on because I truly believed nothing would make this better. My mom definitely would have marched into the school and demanded she be in trouble, and I couldn't take the chance. My dad was a police officer and even if I told him, it wasn't like he could arrest her. I needed to figure this out myself.

I decided this bully had some deep psychological issues going on in her head. It made no sense that after weeks she would bring up the ponytail and just start stalking me for no reason. I knew I was an easy target for her at this point because I wasn't standing up for myself and I wasn't challenging her. I was letting her scare me and she knew it. The more scared I was the more power it gave her. She was taking all my power away from me, and I could feel it. The weeks went on and on and she continued to stalk me. She followed me in the hall saying little weird things behind me. She stared at me through door windows, open doors, across the lunchroom. I continued to avoid her, go right to my classroom, and I was suddenly sick a lot. I skipped days and found myself so afraid to go to school that I would just curl up in a ball and cry. My grades dropped, I was depressed, and I had no appetite. I felt powerless.

Softball season was starting, and I prayed she didn't join the team. This was another sport I excelled at, and I really wanted to finish off my high school career playing. If she joined, there was no doubt in my mind, I would not play. I cautiously went to practice and by the grace of God she didn't join the team. I was able to catch my breath for a minute and enjoy this time after school not in fear of my life for an hour. Friends had been asking me by now what was going on with the bully and me. I had no answers. I said nothing other than *I just don't know*. It seemed by this point it was known around the school that I was her target, and it was just a matter of "when" the fight between us would happen. I told my friends there would be no fight because I don't know how to fight. I could swing my arms and hope for the best, but I knew nothing about fighting;

except for some sibling wrestling matches, I never was in a fight or hit anything. I didn't even know how to make a fist.

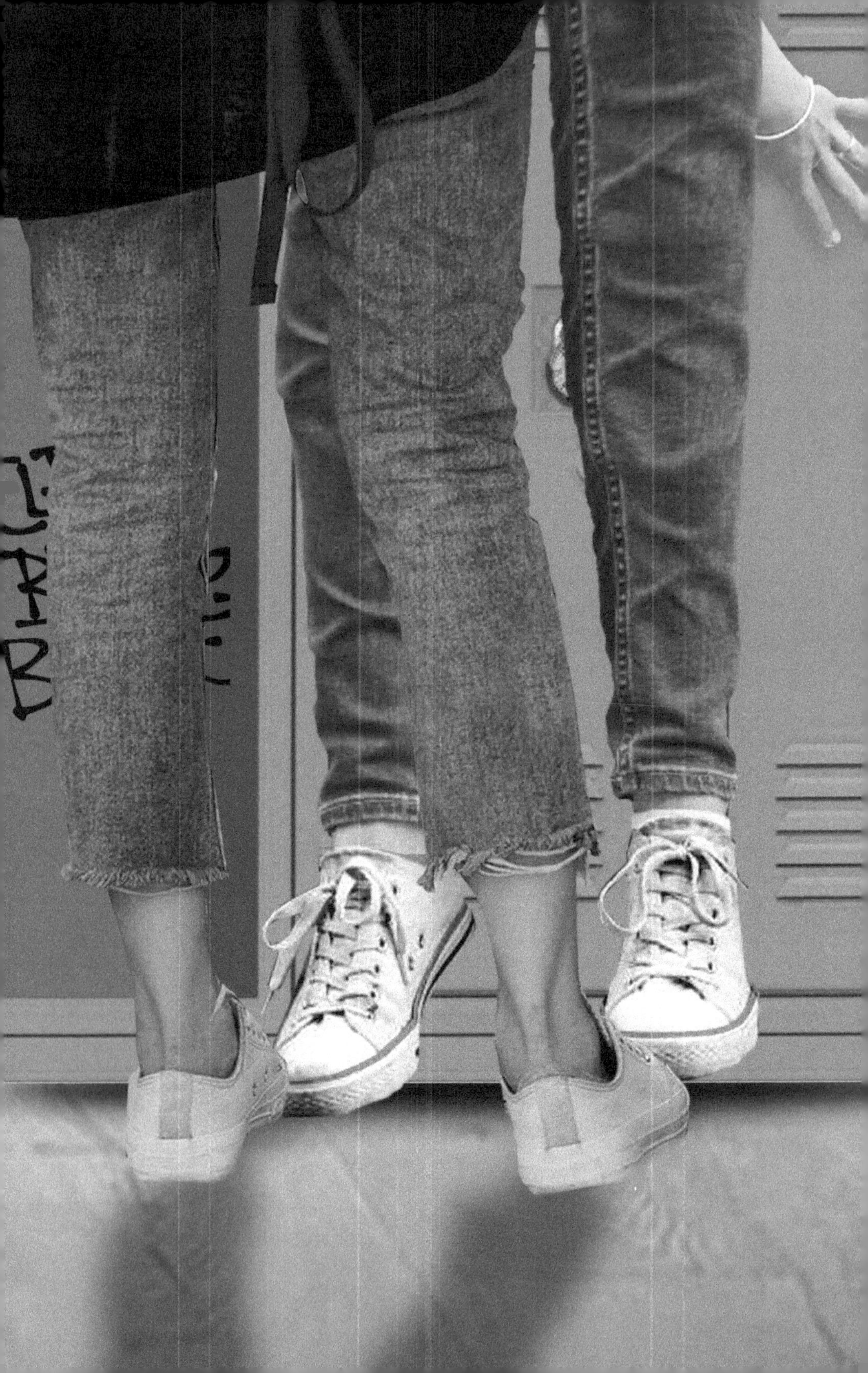

CHAPTER 6
THE LOCKER

Softball practice made me happy. I was starting to feel a little better. I had new friends on the team, practices were really fun, and I was playing awesome. I played left field, but I could catch a ball that was hit anywhere in the outfield. I would run so fast, jump, slide, and do whatever it took to catch those balls. I also loved to bat and would hit triples and homeruns almost every time it was my turn up at bat. I gave some new girls on the softball team a ride to school one morning, and this day was starting off great. I saw no sign of my bully in the parking lot and made it to my locker with no issues. The day went by, and it was quiet.

I had to go to the bathroom so badly during science class and I decided I had to get a pass and take a chance. This made me nervous. I thought, *Well, if anything happens no one will witness it because everyone is in class.* That also meant no one would help me if she was smashing my head into the ground either. I was going to pee myself if I didn't go, so I took the chance. I had my bag with me and asked for the pass. I crept around the corners and made sure the halls were clear.

As I walked towards the bathroom, I saw her. She was walking straight towards me in a rampage. I nervously said, "Hey," and she grabbed me. This was the moment my life flashed before my eyes. I froze in fear. I felt her lift me up off the ground and smash my back against the locker. I couldn't even tell you what she was saying. I felt spit on my face and just heard an angry yelling voice. I totally shut out her words and I didn't even move. The bell rang. Kids came out of the classrooms and saw me pinned up against the locker. I remember seeing faces of the kids. Some were in shock, some were laughing, some gasping. I was frozen as she continued to scream at me while smashing my body like a rag doll against the locker. It was like she was Hercules holding me up with one hand and flicking my head with the other. It felt like this went on for an eternity.

A teacher started to walk over, and she flicked me again and dropped me and walked away. I grabbed my bag that I'd dropped on the floor and ran out of the high school.

I was hyperventilating. I was sobbing, I didn't even know what it was, but I was having a full-blown panic attack. All the anxiety and stress of the last months exploded that day. That moment was scary and embarrassing. I felt ashamed and weak and a million other feelings. I hated life. I hated myself for not being able to fight back or say anything. I hated school. I hated it all. I was consumed with feelings I never felt before and wanted to die.

I had no way to escape all this and had no one helping me. I cried and drove around the back roads, blasting my White Snake cassette tape.

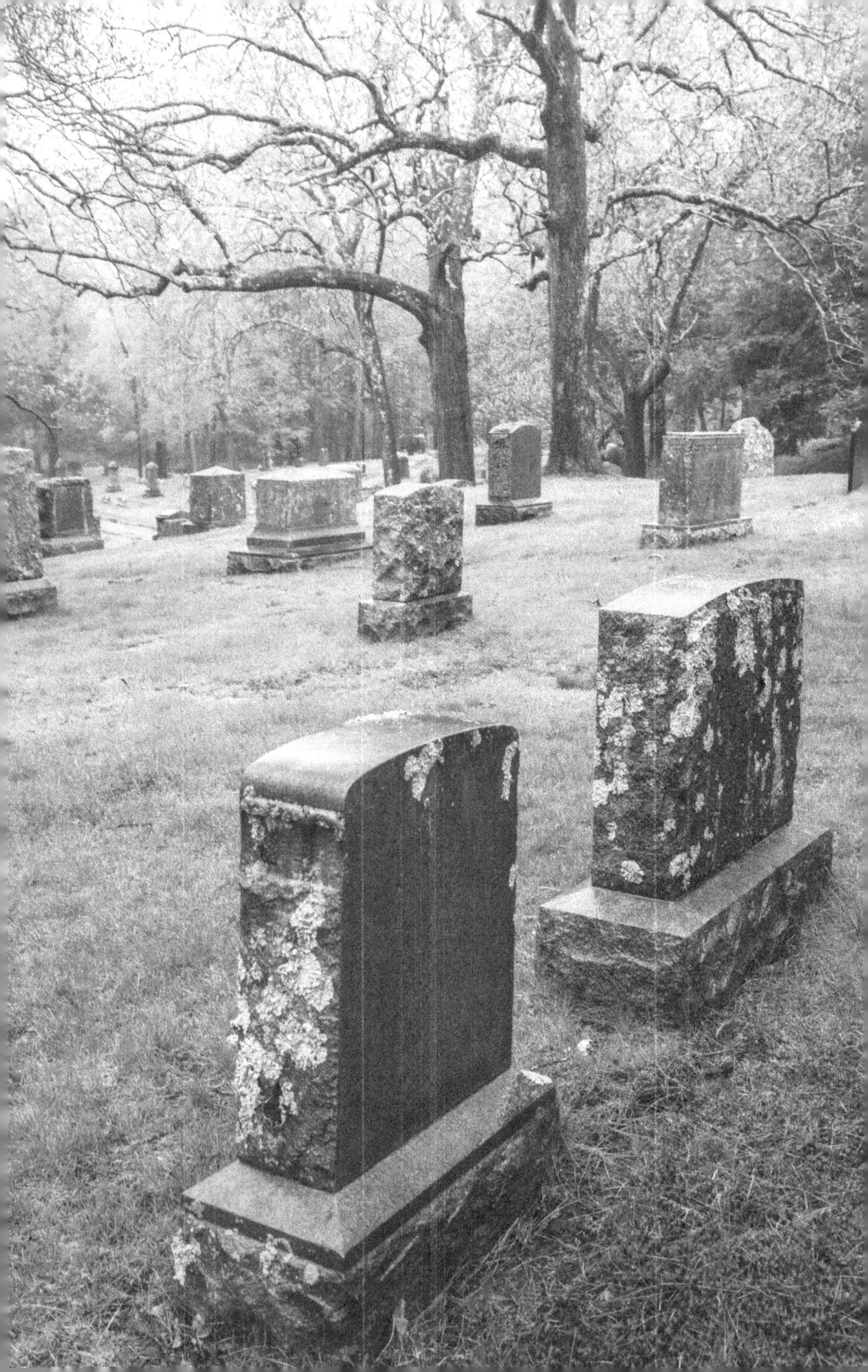

CHAPTER 7
THE CEMETARY

I ended up at the cemetery. There was a beautiful cemetery in the middle of all these corn fields not far from my house. A high school acquaintance died earlier in the school year in a car accident, and she was buried there. I wasn't great friends with her, but I knew her. Some of my other friends knew her better than I did, but when one of your peers dies it hits home. Death becomes real. I decided to park my car here, thinking about this girl, death, and life.

I wanted to die.

I saw in the movies that people could die in their cars, so I was thinking about stuffing my tail pipe and doing that right there in the cemetery. I thought about hanging myself in my basement at home. I thought about cutting my wrists.

All these thoughts made me feel like I'd be free. Free of the torment, the stalking, the name calling, the fear that came along with waking up every single day I went to school.

I was tired of it. I couldn't do it anymore.

I refused to go to school again, and I just wanted to die. Thinking of death felt like freedom.

Then I thought about my sister, brother, mom, dad, grandpa, and grandma. I thought about my friends and how much fun we had. How much I loved my family. How sad Grandma would be if I died.

I didn't really want to die.

I wanted to be free of this bully.

The feeling that this bully brought to my life. I wanted to be free of the anxiety, the torment, the depression. I wanted to be free of the fear this bully brought to me. Why was I allowing this bully to take my power?

I walked around the car; I was standing under a big, beautiful tree. I was just looking around at how beautiful the landscape was. Green grass, golden cornfields, blue skies with big, puffy, white clouds. The birds were chirping and flying all around; the sun was warm on my face.

I didn't really want to die.

I yelled, "GOD! What do I do?! Help me! Please help me! What do I do?"

I don't know who was listening or who helped me, but as I sat there and looked around, wiping tears flowing down my face, I decided to take my power back.

I loved my family. I loved my friends. I loved my life. I wasn't going to let this bully take this away from me. Why was I going to let her win? Why would I die for her?

I said, "Christina, you have the power! Take your power back!" Yes, I spoke to myself and told myself to take my power back.

What was I afraid of? Well, first off, I was afraid of her beating me up. The second thing I was afraid of was being embarrassed in front of all my peers. That's it. Just two things I was afraid of.

I decided I needed to learn how to fight.

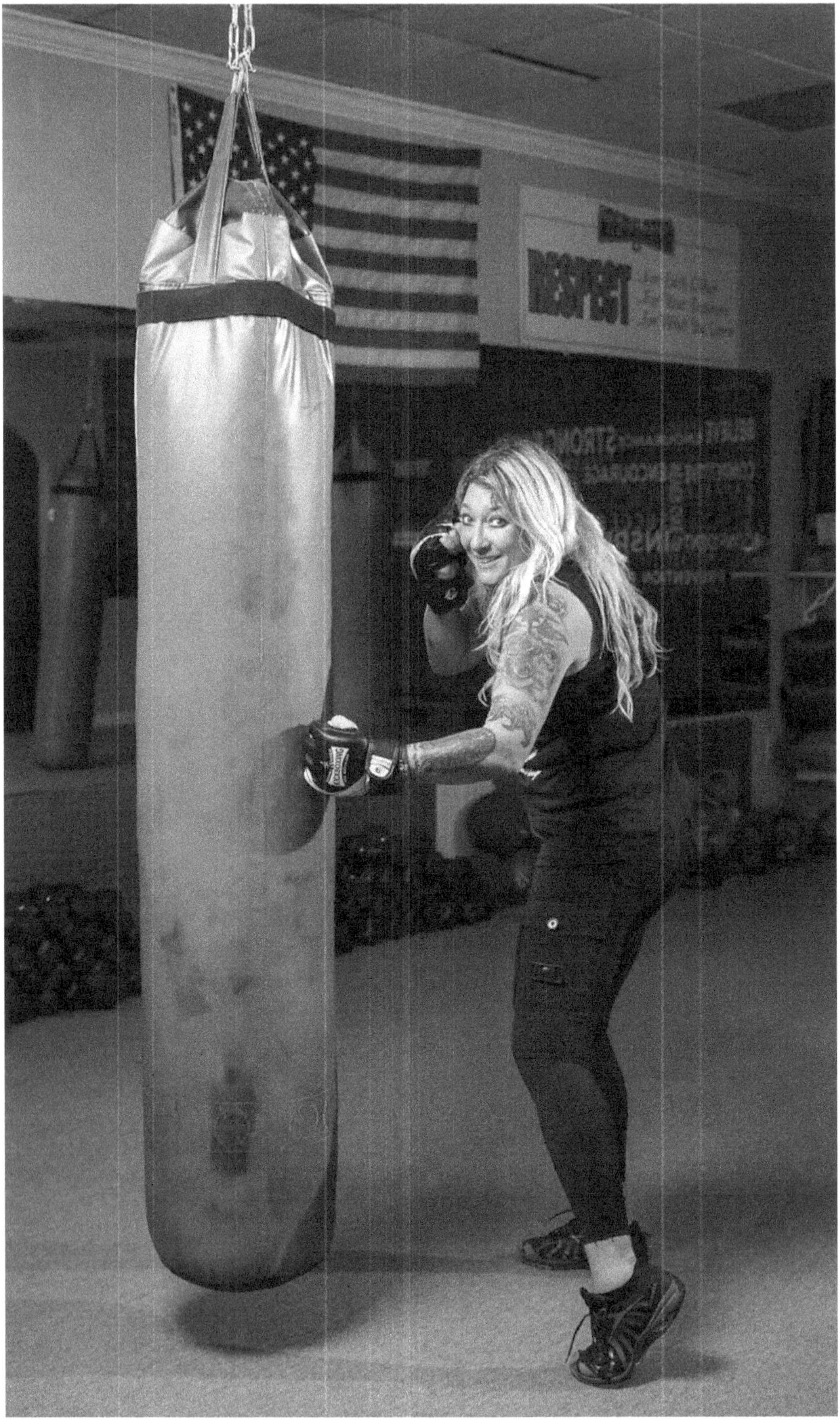
RESPECT

CHAPTER 8
ROCKY

I loved the *Rocky* movies. I decided I was going to train and learn how to fight like Rocky. I went home and asked my dad if we could get a heavy bag and if he could show me how to punch. Dad agreed, and within a few days he hung a heavy bag in our basement and gave me some bag gloves. He showed me how to make a fist and I started punching the heavy bag. I worked out in my basement doing everything I saw Rocky do in the movies, and if I'd had a chicken, I would have chased that too. I went and bought big black boots and decided if she touched me again, I would kick her with big boots. I wore clothes I would be comfortable in to fight when I went to school and was telling myself I could do this. I was determined to fight back next time she put her hands on me.

A few weeks went by, and the bully wasn't around. I was relieved but never knew when she would return so I always kept my guard up. I still had bad anxiety and depression, and I hated everything, but I was trying hard to not let this consume me.

After softball practice one day, all the girls were wrestling and play fighting in my yard. One girl took out some sparring equipment and was showing us her kicks and punches. I wrestled with her, and she swept my foot and threw me over her hip with ease. I asked her how she knew how to do that, and she told me she took karate class with her dad. I was so intrigued.

I never thought of taking karate class. I saw *The Karate Kid* movies but apparently, I liked Rocky better and thought Rocky was the way to go.

I started to get very excited about the thought of knowing karate and how to kick. She told me she would give me a free lesson pass. I was so excited but very nervous. I nervously went to the karate school one night for my free lesson. I was met by a Sensei with a black belt on. He handed me a Gi and pointed to the changing room. I came out with this giant white Gi on and felt pretty silly. He went over all the rules. No shoes in the dojo, bow in and out, and no talking in class. I followed along with the warmup, and then he had an advanced student help me with some basic moves.

I loved it. I felt amazing after the karate class and couldn't wait to come back again.

I went home and talked to my parents. I asked my dad if he would pay for the fee for me to join for a month and he said, "No. You won't stick with it." That motivated me to prove him wrong. I somehow (probably Mom) came up with the money and joined karate. As I took classes, I fell in love with all of it: the respect, the discipline, the moves, point fighting, katas, and weapons. I started going to competitions and competing. I learned how to do point fighting and my feet became lethal weapons. I was good at it, and I wanted to learn more.

I competed in sport karate competitions all over the world. I was so good at fighting I was getting disqualified during point fighting for excessive contact. I was told about WAKO fighting, which was a step up from point karate fighting. I learned about a kickboxing trainer and boxing trainer in my home state of Rhode Island and decided to learn from both of them to make myself even better. I went on to join the USA Kickboxing team, and I fought WAKO in Ireland, Italy, and Poland. I did continuous fighting, started teaching little kids at my karate school, and the next thing I know my life took an entire direction that I never even dreamed of.

While I was taking Karate, my confidence and self-esteem built up more than I ever could have imagined. I was a new person. I wasn't scared anymore. I had no fear and felt no anxiety or stress. The depression lifted, I had my appetite back, and I was happy. I was so happy and enjoying life.

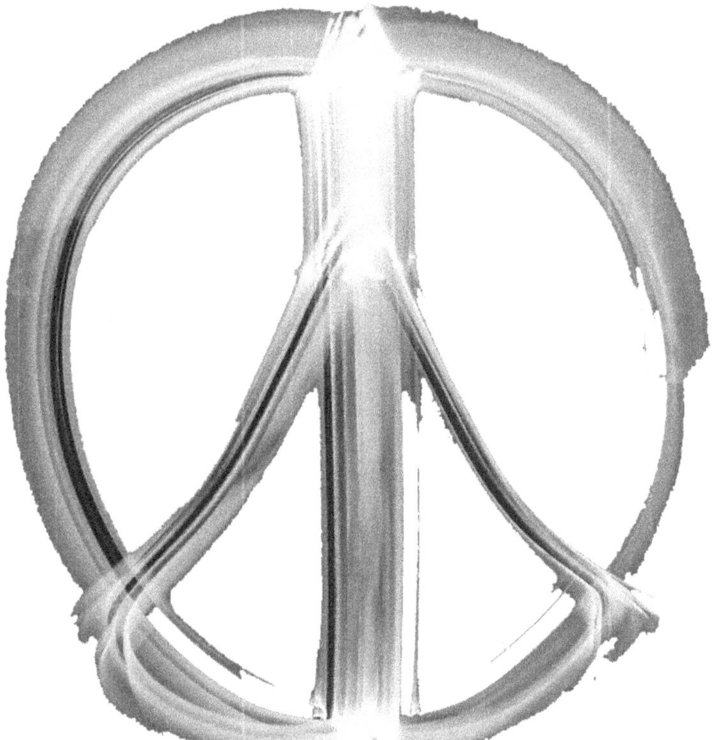

CHAPTER 9
BYE-BYE BULLY

Just like that, the bully disappeared. As my confidence grew, and the senior year came to an end, she vanished. Nothing ever happened again. She didn't stalk me; I saw her randomly here and there but that was it. No digs, no comments... gone.

Bye-bye bully. If she did return, I was ready for her; I was ready to stand up and take her flicks and hits and spit in my face. I was ready to get my power back.

I think back to how I wanted to end my life because of this bully. I am so happy I didn't let those feelings overcome me. I am so blessed that something inside me – or call it divine intervention – interceded and gave me the feeling to fight.

Fight and take my power back and never let anyone take my power from me again. I realized those feelings of wanting to die were feelings in that moment, a buildup, and as horrible and sad as they felt, I fought through them. I knew I didn't really want to die. I just needed hope, a solution to the problem. I found the courage inside myself to learn how to fight, and that alone gave me the confidence I needed to be who I am today.

I truly believe that if we can give kids who are victims of bullies the confidence to defend themselves, they have a better chance to fight through all the stress, anxiety, and depression that comes along with being bullied. Along with that confidence they find their voice. They find something inside themselves that makes them find their inner power. They will find their power, and once you find your power you won't let anyone ever take it from you again. I know this from experience.

I am not saying *violence* is the answer; I am saying *confidence* is the answer. We gain confidence by having control of our situations. A bully takes your power from you by fear of violence and being physical, so if a child knows how to fight and defend themselves, a bully can't take that from them. Then that child won't be a target of that bully. A bully won't pick on someone who can fight back or someone they know they will lose a fight against. Because of my own experience and over 33 years of teaching martial arts and kickboxing, listening to hundreds of stories about kids being bullied, I can confidently say that giving a child the life skill of learning how to fight will be one of the best gifts you can give.

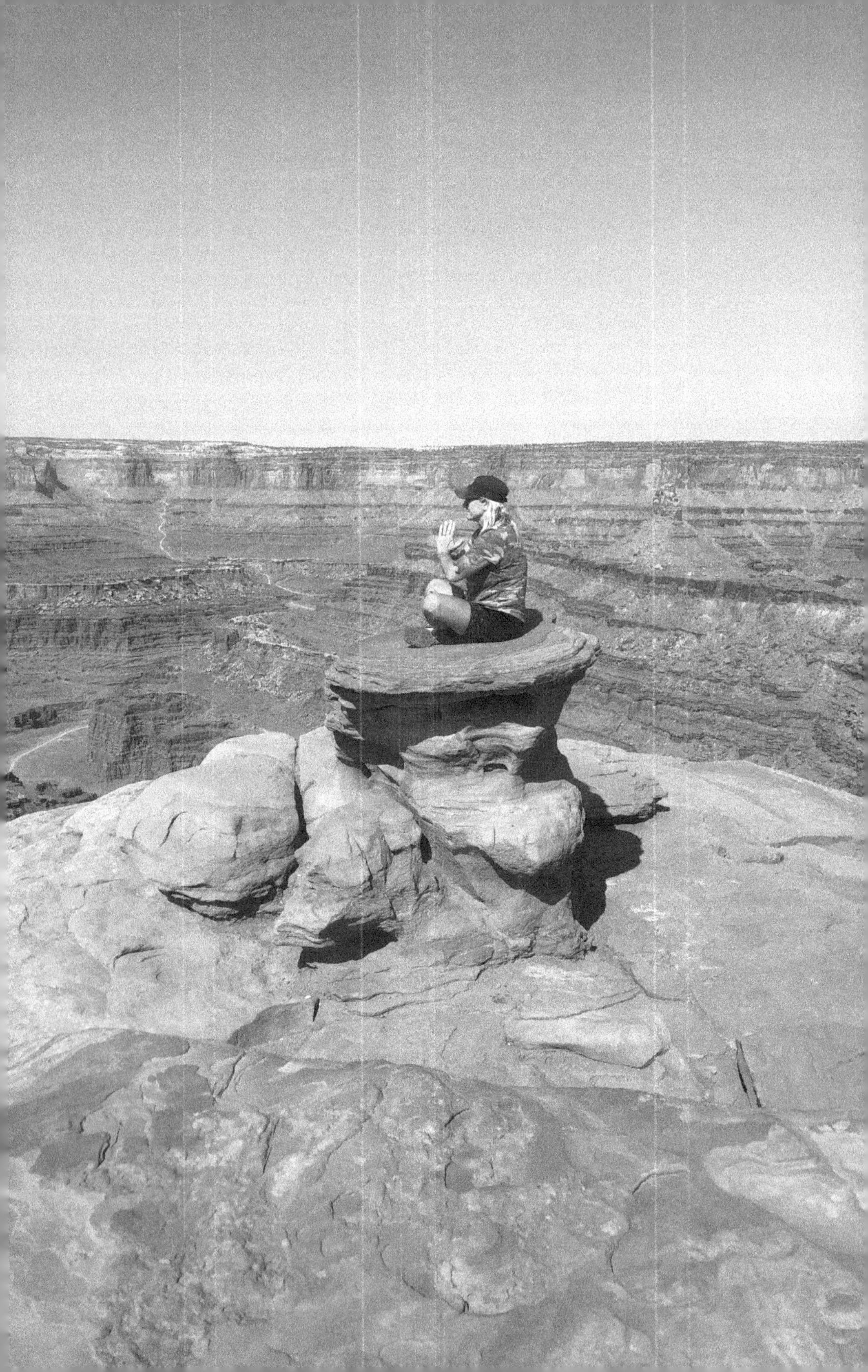

CHAPTER 10
MY BULLY'S BLESSINGS TO ME

I reflect and can truly say, "Wow."

If it wasn't for that bully and what it pushed me to feel and do, I wouldn't be the person I am today. Because of my experience, I learned how to fight, and fighting turned into my life. For over 33 years I have taught kids martial arts, kids' kickboxing, adult kickboxing, boxing, fight teams, and personal training. I hold a 5th degree black belt, I fought sport karate which took me all over the world competing in tournaments, I then joined the USA WAKO KB team and went to 3 countries – Italy, Ireland, and Poland. I was fighting amateur kickboxing and then was asked to turn Professional. I turned Professional Kickboxer and had fights on Pay Per View and was then was asked to be on the Maury Povich show titled "You Can't Believe What I Do For a Living." Cosmopolitan magazine picked me as one of their fun, fearless, females and brought me to NYC to mingle with celebrities and celebrate all of us top 10 fun, fearless, females in the USA. I filmed a kickboxing video that was sold on TV (VHS tape) called Fitness Kickboxing: The Real Workout. I was asked to be in three music videos as a fighter. I fought Pro Boxing, and was the first female boxing match in the state of New Hampshire. I was then picked up by Chuck Norris and asked to be the only female on Team New England for his World Combat League Team. I retired after that fight with a sellout crowd at Mohegan Sun Casino Arena. I opened my own Kickboxing school as a teen, and I was able to change other people's lives, giving them the gift of confidence.

This is not a career path I could have ever dreamed of, and if anyone ever told me I was going to be a fighter I would have laughed hysterically. But here I am. My life became fighting and kickboxing. I am blessed by the unexpected gifts of my bully; my bully gave me everything she took away.

I have had a life of freedom, confidence, and amazing self-esteem.

Don't let anyone ever take your power away.

> "You have the power to create
> the life you want."
> **– CHRISTINA RONDEAU**

BULLYING

Bullying comes down to two basic things.

1. The fear of being HIT.

2. The fear of being embarrassed in front of friends.

Bullying can be defined as repeated aggressive behavior that is intended to cause harm, distress, or fear in another person. It involves an imbalance of power, where the person who bullies uses their position or strength to intimidate or dominate the target. Bullying can take various forms, such as physical, verbal, or psychological, and it often occurs repeatedly over a period of time.

It's important to note that bullying is not limited to just physical acts of aggression. It can also include spreading rumors, exclusion, cyberbullying (using technology to harm or harass others), or any action that intentionally undermines someone's well-being and self-esteem. Bullies may target individuals based on their appearance, race, gender, sexual orientation, disabilities, or any other perceived difference.

Bullying has serious negative effects on the person being bullied, including emotional distress, low self-esteem, anxiety, panic attacks, depression, failed grades, physical health problems, and even push a person to suicide. If we can get rid of these two fears, we can really help change the dynamic and help the person to not be a victim of a bully.

Have you ever seen a strong, confident person who doesn't give a care about what other people say about them be bullied?

No – you probably haven't.

These people are not afraid of being hit. They probably can fight and feel confident in their ability to defend themselves. They are also outspoken and won't allow someone to talk down to them, therefore they won't be embarrassed in front of friends because they have good self-esteem and feel more powerful than the bully.

BULLYING INFORMATION SHEET TO HELP PARENTS

RECOMMENDATIONS FOR PARENTS

1. Find out if your school has a bullying form and fill it out. Some are online.

2. Go to the school committee meetings.

3. Attend the school improvement meetings.

4. Request a meeting with the superintendent / send an email.

5. Talk to the school resource officer – calmly.

6. Paper trail! Report any cyber bullying to the state police. They have a cyber bullying unit.

7. Be persistent but polite and keep ADVOCATING that something is done.

8. Get an IEP or 504 plan for your child so you can get special accommodation in place if needed.

9. YOU NEED to have an advocate with you at the meetings that fully comprehends the language used for IEP and 504 plans. Ask the special education department for an advocate.

Every school is required to have an anti-bullying policy in place, and it is submitted to the department of education.

A parent can request a copy of it.

UNDERSTANDING WHAT BULLYING IS FROM A TEACHER'S PERSPECTIVE

This is from a teacher's perspective - they see 2 major problems:

1.   People seem unclear about what bullying is. It must be targeted and repeated to be considered bullying. Some kid not liking your kid's new shoes is not bullying. Kids are mean and unfiltered but they're not all bullies.

2.   No one wants to give names! They need to tell the teachers/authorities *who* the bully is and exactly *what* they are doing. Teachers don't see it happening because bullies are sneaky, and even if the teacher can guess they still need the parent or child to tell them – *and be specific* – so they can put an act upon it.

*** Parents think it will get worse if they tell and then they blame the teachers for not doing anything. Teachers can't randomly accuse a kid without specifics.

PARENTS, SUPPORT YOUR CHILDREN THROUGH THIS TOUGH TIME

** Remember, your child is going through a difficult time.

They need mental and emotional support from you.

Teach them good, healthy coping skills in this time so they don't turn to unhealthy coping skills such as vaping, cutting, drugs, etc.

They need to have an outlet and to know they are safe to talk about it.

Remember, sometimes just HOLDING SPACE and LISTENING TO THEM is all they need.

They may just want to vent, so just LISTEN. Sometimes, anything you say will be "wrong" because you are a safe target for them to be mad at and get angry at. Just remember it's not you. You're just safe to take it out on.

HERE ARE SOME THINGS YOU CAN DO AS A PARENT TO HELP YOUR CHILD:

1. Create an open and trusting environment: Encourage your child to talk about their experiences and feelings. Let them know that you're there to listen and support them without judgment.

2. Empower your child: Help your child build self-esteem and self-confidence by focusing on their strengths and positive qualities. Encourage them to participate in activities they enjoy and excel in, which can boost their self-worth.

3. Teach assertiveness skills: Teach your child how to stand up for themselves in a non-confrontational way. Role-playing different scenarios can be helpful in practicing assertive responses.

4. Establish communication with the school: Reach out to your child's teacher, principal, or counselor to discuss

the situation. Ask about their anti-bullying policies and measures in place. Collaborate with the school to develop a plan to ensure your child's safety.

5. Encourage friendships: Help your child foster healthy relationships with their peers. Encourage them to join clubs, sports teams, or other activities where they can meet like-minded individuals and form friendships.

6. Teach coping strategies: Equip your child with effective coping strategies, such as deep breathing exercises, journaling, or engaging in hobbies they enjoy. These techniques can help alleviate stress and anxiety caused by bullying.

7. Seek professional help if needed: If the bullying persists or your child's emotional well-being is significantly affected, consider seeking professional help from a therapist or counselor who specializes in working with children.

Remember, it's essential to approach the situation with empathy and patience. Let your child know that you are on their side, and that together, you will find a solution.

HERE IS A LIST OF SUGGESTIONS TO HELP YOU AS THE PARENT OF A BULLIED CHILD

1. School resources: Start by reaching out to your child's school. Many schools have anti-bullying policies and programs in place. You can talk to the principal, counselor, or teacher to discuss the situation and learn about the resources available within the school.

2. Parent support groups: Look for local or online support groups specifically for parents of bullied children. These groups provide a safe space for parents to share their experiences, seek advice, and offer support to one another.

3. Helplines and hotlines: There are helplines and hotlines dedicated to supporting parents dealing with bullying. These resources can provide guidance, information, and emotional support. Look for helplines specific to your country or region.

4. Online resources: Many organizations and websites offer valuable information and resources for parents dealing with bullying. Websites like StopBullying.gov, PACER's National Bullying Prevention Center, and Stomp Out Bullying provide resources, tips, and strategies for parents.

5. Professional counseling or therapy: If you feel the need for additional support, consider seeking help from a professional counselor or therapist. They can provide guidance, help your child develop coping strategies, and offer support to both you and your child.

6. Enroll your child in a self-defense/martial arts, karate, krav maga, boxing, or kickboxing program. Your children need to feel confident and increase their self-esteem. These programs will help them with both while giving them the skills to defend themselves physically against a bully. Remember to visit and take a free class at a few different places before deciding on the right one for you and your child. Not all instructors are the same, so find one that is the right fit.

Remember that it's important to tailor the resources to your specific situation and seek professional advice when necessary.

SELF-CARE FOR YOU AND YOUR CHILD/REN

Parents, navigating these times is undeniably challenging. Please remember to pause, breathe, and prioritize your well-being. Embracing self-care is crucial, especially when surrounded by negativity. It's essential not only for your own equilibrium, but also as a positive model for your children. They, too, will benefit from constructive outlets and coping mechanisms. Consult the following list to guide both of you in selecting effective and positive coping skills.

Here's a list of positive coping skills people can use during stressful times:

1. **Deep Breathing**: Taking slow, deep breaths can calm the nervous system.

2. **Exercise**: Physical activity releases endorphins which act as natural painkillers and mood elevators.

3. **Journaling**: Writing down feelings can provide a safe outlet for emotions.

4. **Mindfulness Meditation**: Helps keep one grounded and present in the moment.

5. **Guided Imagery**: Visualizing calming scenarios can reduce anxiety and stress.

6. **Progressive Muscle Relaxation**: Systematically tensing and then relaxing muscle groups can relieve physical tension.

7. **Yoga**: Combines physical postures with deep breathing and meditation.

8. **Listening to Music**: Music can be therapeutic and alter one's mood.

9. **Reading**: Getting lost in a book can be a form of escapism.

10. **Engaging in Hobbies**: Doing something enjoyable can distract from stress and increase feelings of accomplishment.

11. **Connecting with Others**: Talking to someone trusted can provide support and a different perspective.

12. **Limiting Caffeine and Sugar**: Reducing intake can

help decrease feelings of jitteriness and anxiety.

13. **Adequate Sleep**: Ensuring you get enough rest is vital for mental and emotional well-being.

14. **Nature Walks**: Spending time in nature has been shown to reduce feelings of stress.

15. **Limiting Screen Time**: Taking breaks from screens can reduce mental fatigue.

16. **Laughing**: Whether it's watching a comedy or chatting with a funny friend, laughter is therapeutic.

17. **Positive Affirmations**: Replacing negative thoughts with positive affirmations can shift mindset.

18. **Artistic Expression**: Drawing, painting, or crafting can be therapeutic outlets.

19. **Setting Boundaries**: Knowing when to say no or take a break can prevent burnout.

20. **Time Management**: Organizing tasks and breaking them into manageable steps can reduce feelings of overwhelm.

21. **Seeking Professional Help**: If stress becomes unmanageable, seeking help from a therapist or counselor can be beneficial.

22. **Gratitude Journaling**: Focusing on positive aspects and things you're grateful for can shift perspective.

23. **Limiting Alcohol**: While it may seem relaxing, alcohol can increase feelings of anxiety and stress in the long run.

24. **Pet Therapy**: Spending time with animals can be calming.

25. **Avoiding Procrastination**: Breaking tasks into smaller steps and tackling them can prevent last-minute stress.

26. **Grounding Techniques**: Methods like the "5-4-3-2-1" technique can help divert focus from anxiety and ground you in the present.

27. **Learning to Let Go**: Understanding what's in your control and what isn't can help reduce unnecessary stress.

28. **Scheduled Breaks**: Taking regular breaks during work or study can help maintain a fresh mind.

29. **Massage**: Relaxes tense muscles and provides a feeling of relaxation.

30. **Hydration and Balanced Diet**: Drinking enough water and eating balanced meals can help maintain physical and mental health.

Remember, everyone is different. What works as a coping mechanism for one person might not necessarily work for another. It's essential to find what resonates with you personally and practice those skills regularly.